Pebble® Plus

BARN OWLS

by Melissa Hill

raintree
a Capstone company — publishers for children

Raintree is an imprint of Capstone Global Library Limited, a company incorporated in England and Wales having its registered office at 7 Pilgrim Street, London, EC4V 6LB – Registered company number: 6695582

www.raintree.co.uk
myorders@raintree.co.uk

Editorial Credits
Jeni Wittrock, editor; Juliette Peters, designer; Morgan Walters, media researcher; Katy LaVigne, production specialist

ISBN 978 1 4747 0495 3
19 18 17 16 15
10 9 8 7 6 5 4 3 2 1

British Library Cataloguing in Publication Data
A full catalogue record for this book is available from the British Library.

Photo Credits
Dreamstime: Steve Allen, 17; Getty Images: Berndt Fischer, 11, Steve Maslowski, 19; Glow Images: Manfred Danegger/Corbis, 15; iStockphoto: iculizard, 21; Shutterstock: Andrew Astbury, 7, Artography, (bark design) throughout, 3, Dennis W. Donohue, 1, 9, J. Helgason, 2, 24, jadimages, 13, John C Evans, 3, Patrick Rolands, 22, Philip Ellard, cover, Sean Pavone, (background) 1, 2, 23, 24, Valerio Pardi,

Printed in China

Contents

Shriek in the night

Hiss! What was that? It was a barn owl. Barn owls do not hoot the way other owls do. These pale owls shriek and hiss.

Worldly owls

Barn owls live near open fields and deserts. They are often found inside empty buildings such as barns. That is how they got their name.

Barn owls are rarely seen during the day. But they live all over the world. Barn owls live on every continent except Antarctica.

North America

Europe

Asia

Africa

South America

Australia

where barn owls live

Hungry hunters

Barn owls are raptors.

These flying hunters weigh

0.5 kilograms (1 pound).

Their wings stretch out

1.1 metres (3.5 feet).

Size comparison

barn owl
length:
33–41 centimetres
(13–16 inches)

budgie
length:
15–20 centimetres
(6–8 inches)

Barn owls are nocturnal.
In the dark they hunt prey
by listening. Their heart-shaped
faces catch sounds made by
small animals.

An owl flies towards the sound of its prey. Its long legs stretch out. The owl grabs the mouse with its talons.

A barn owl can eat 1,000 mice in a year. They also eat other rodents, rabbits and small birds. In the wild, barn owls can live for 10 years or more.

Family to feed

Barn owls need to be good hunters. They have large families to feed! They may have as many as nine chicks each year.

After two months, barn owl
chicks can fly. Soon they
will be hunting, too.

GLOSSARY

continent one of Earth's seven large land masses

hiss make a "sss" sound like a snake

nocturnal active at night and resting during the day

predator animal that hunts other animals for food

prey animal that is hunted by other animals for food

raptor bird of prey that hunts and eats other animals, catching them with their feet

rodent one of a group of small mammals with large front teeth for chewing

shriek high scream or call

talon long, sharp, curved claw

READ MORE

Barn Owls (Night Safari), Rebecca Rissman (Raintree, 2014)

Birds (Animal Classification), Angela Royston (Raintree, 2015)

Owl vs Mouse (Predator vs Prey), Mary Meinking Chambers (Raintree, 2012)

WEBSITES

The Barn Owl Trust
www.barnowltrust.org.uk

BBC Nature: barn owl videos, news and facts
www.bbc.co.uk/nature/life/Barn_Owl

COMPREHENSION QUESTIONS

1. Barn owls live for 10 years in the wild. Why might barn owls live longer in a zoo or bird sanctuary?

2. Owls are raptors. Raptors are birds that catch prey using their feet. What other birds might be raptors?

INDEX